Our New Baby

written by BETH ATCHISON
illustrated by NANCY MUNGER

The Standard Publishing Company, Cincinnati, Ohio. A division of Standex International Corporation.
Text © 1999 by Beth Atchison. Illustrations © 1999 by The Standard Publishing Company.
Cover design by Matt Key.
Printed in the United States of America. All rights reserved.

06 05 04 03 02 01 00 99   5 4 3 2 1

Library of Congress Catalog Card Number 98-61294
ISBN 0-7847-0894-0
Scripture on page 24 quoted from the *International Children's Bible, New Century Version,*
© 1986, 1988 by Word Publishing, Dallas, Texas 75039.
Used by permission.

STANDARD
PUBLISHING
Cincinnati, Ohio

Mama told me a secret.
She patted her tummy.
"Our new baby's inside,"
she told me, "but not for long."
I had lots of questions.
"Will I have a sister or
a brother? Will I have to
share my toys? I want to
be a baby, too. Can I?"

Mama smiled. "God is sending us this special baby," she said. "God sent you when you were a baby. You are very special, too."

Mama said I'll always be special even though I'm not a baby anymore. We prayed, "Dear God, thank you for our new baby you are sending us."

For a while, Mama ate a lot of crackers. She said they helped her tummy feel better.

Daddy helped get the dinners. He's a good cook, but we like frozen dinners the best.

Daddy let me set the table. I got everything just right. Daddy said he's proud of me.

We prayed, "Dear God, let us be good helpers for Mama."

Soon the baby wasn't a secret anymore.
"Our new baby's inside," Mama said, "but
not for long!" I touched my Mama's tummy.
It looked like Mama was getting fat!

As the baby grew, Mama needed extra rest. When she took a nap, I tried to play very quietly.

I like to draw pictures. I drew one for Mama. I prayed, "Dear God, help Mama feel better."

Mama was hungry all the time. She fixed dinner. She fixed snacks. She sent Daddy and me out to buy her a milk shake. We all had strawberry milk shakes.

Mama looked happy. She hummed pretty songs. Daddy patted her round tummy every time he gave her a hug. They said it would be great having a little baby at our house again. Because I'm big, I will be the big helper. That's an important job! I prayed, "Dear God, thank you for my special job."

I helped Mama turn the guest room into a nursery. Mama got out all my baby clothes. "You used to be so tiny!" she said, as she held up a little shirt. It was small enough to fit my teddy bear.

I couldn't believe that I was ever that small!

We looked at pictures of me when I was a baby. I've grown a lot! Our new baby will grow, too. Someday, our baby will be big enough to play with me.

I prayed, "Dear God, thanks for helping the baby and me grow."

Mama said I needed lots of care when I was tiny.
Our new baby will need lots of care, too. I asked,
"How can I help the tiny baby?"

Mama said, "There are lots of things you can do!" She said that I could sing to the baby and make the baby laugh. I could get the baby's bottle and even help change the diapers! But I think I will let Mama and Daddy do that!

Mama lost her lap. There was nowhere left for me to sit. Daddy let me sit on his lap instead. But I still wanted Mama's lap. Sometimes she held me on her knees.

Mama said she would have a lap again when the baby was born. Daddy said, "Then you can sit on Mama's lap and help her hold the baby."

We prayed, "Dear God, help me share my Mama with our new baby."

"Our new baby's jumping inside," Daddy and I said, "but not for long!" We looked at Mama's tummy. It was so big, I hoped it would not POP! I felt the baby kick. What a surprise!

Mama packed her suitcase to take to the hospital.
She said our new baby would be born very soon.

I felt lonely when Daddy and Mama left to go
to the hospital. But Grandma came to take care of
me. We read lots of books, and I liked snuggling
in Grandma's lap.

She prayed with me,
"Dear God, keep Mama
and Daddy safe while
our new baby is born."

Soon the phone rang. It was Daddy. He told me the news. My baby sister was born! Daddy said she was beautiful. And wow, was she loud!

When Daddy and Mama came home with the baby, they were so proud of her. They were proud of me, too, and gave me a big hug.

My sister looked wrinkly and very small. Daddy said she looked a lot like me. I didn't think so.

We all prayed, "Dear God, thank you for our new baby."

Now I am a big brother. I like my sister
even if she is a little noisy sometimes.
I help take care of her.

When someone comes to see the baby in her room, I show the way.

I like to say, "Shhhh! Our new baby sleeps inside—"

"But not for long!"

Serve each other with love.
Galatians 5:13